Scene of the Crime

Scene

of the

Crime

Poems
by
Jane Ransom

Story Line Press
1997

Published by Story Line Press, Inc.
Three Oaks Farm
Brownsville, OR 97327

Text design by Stacy Rathbun
Cover design by Chiquita Babb

This publication was made possible thanks in part to the generous
support of the Nicholas Roerich Museum, the Andrew W. Mellon
Foundation and our individual contributors.

Library of Congress Cataloging-in-Publication Data

Ransom, Jane Reavill, 1958-
    Scene of the Crime: poems/ by Jane Reavill Ransom.
        p.   cm.
    ISBN 1-885266-56-1
    1. Crime--Poetry.   I. Title.
PS3568.A579S28   1997
813' .54--cd21
                                                    97-17496
                                                        CIP

acknowledgements

Black Swan Review:

"Authority, Don't Give Me that Archaic Smile"
"Letter of Explanation"
"Mr. America Visits Sex-Surrogate Miss History"

Eidos:

"Citizen Jane"

Generator:

"The Imp...e Rides Again"
"My Idle Idyll Essence"
"Criminal Confession"
"Crap-Trap"

Lingo: A Journal of the Arts:

"Self Delphinitions"
"Color by Number"
"But It Will"
"'Self-Help,' a Two-Act Play"
"Domestic Bliss"

Negative Capability:

"Shift: A Woman's Chemise or a Dress"

New York Quarterly:

"See, Saw, Scene of the Crime"

Open 24 Hours:

"Good Advice"

Poetry New York:

"Pussycat"

Private Arts:

"Ground Rules"
"Hot Cross Bun"

Sojourner:

"Prayer"

Whiskey Island Magazine:

"Yowling for Blood"

for
michael mandler

contents

ground rules

You can heckle,
You can jeckle, but you can't hide.
A bitch in rhyme saves time.
A bird in the hand means
"Screw you."
Screw you? Excuse me — my, my
Grammar and cycle: O
Be my reader, reader,
Author-eater. Read my life
But don't you be her. Put me in a paradigm
And there you'll keep me for some time —
Being's time-been. Soon you will be mine again.
Don't put the start before the source.
Slow down, take my time.
Walk, don't run
On...
Talk; don't sit
Tight at the end of the funnel. Relax,
Let it all doubt.
Do be fickle, but don't be snide.
A witch in lines raves, whines.
A bird in the hand is worth two
Loose screws. Screws youse.
Excuse meeze.
Three blind dice. See how they roll.
They all go after Adam's wife,
Who cuts off their tales with a piece of advice:
Get her safe, then sorry.
Play it again, Lamb
Stew, all you want to.
You can snicker but you have to abide.
A switch in signs changes mine.
A bird in the hand is mirth to
You. You there. There, there's
A fork in the ode,
A sop in the Beckett.
I before me, except to "be."
And you. *Love you.*

1

bye
mom

see, saw, scene of the crime

See Saw. Girl goes down. Boy goes up. Boy goes down. Boy gets
   off. Girl goes down,
Girl gets off. I killed my mother. It's every girl's dream;
I did it to my mother.

Jungle Gyms. Fist by fist. Chin up. Feet helpless. Hold on.
Move it. Finish
Before my arms give out; give my arms
Up now. Hugsy-wugsy.

Swing. Seat in the bucket. From him to her to him to her to him to —
Gravity will stop me in the middle.
Wanna screw Mommy and Daddy. Can't choose.

Merry-Go-Round. Sluggish first, barely speaking as the groins spin. Spoke,
Star rays in a circle — nip-hole. Twirling while the girl
Screams: I did so kill my mother.

Slide. After the ladder up, the wait thrusts me down — knees
Slam concrete. Bloody hands and feet. I gave her the morphine. She
   begged me —
Too, it's every girl's dream come true.

but it will

Right off you should understand I want to kill
And eat my mother. Only she's already dead,
So I masturbate instead. Today a woman's hand spread into a bird
Which flew across the table to my snailed fist
And alit in a sympathetic gesture. I was stunned
And moved by her naiveté. I reached out
And shut her jeans' top snap. Days later
I burst into tears. That has not happened yet,
But it will; I'm a sex-acts murderess.
My body-stuffed lawn leaks blood. For closure,
Each story ends by sacrifice, a heart
Dying in my clench. Oh, oh, I'm losing my grip. Look God, no hands! as I write
By licking the stenographer's ear. My hands disappeared digging graves
In my panties and brassiere. Look hands, no God. Now who will dictate
My sentence? Watch me model guilt — deposing as a big swine, a little suckling
At the world's breast. I long for the pork-chop-chop rhythm
Of a slaughterhouse. Every baby's naturally a cannibal. Eat, eat, be eaten.
Up with all-consuming! Matricidal fantasies? Spanky clean
As Ivory, my "conscience" is an mmm-oral construct. And it floats.
I love dead-baby jokes. Or a good dead-mommy hoax. Oooo yes I do, I love

My mother who, like so many, is neither here nor there
Being all those bodies lodged in my underwear. At birth I was slapped
With someone's summons for oral parody;
They claimed I cried just like my mother. How was I
To differ? Re- Re- Re-enact, gently down the stream
Of conscientiousness. I do. I do. I do. I am monogamous
Every time, like Mark Twain quitting cigarettes. I don't hold back or front
For anyone. I need victimizer's therapy; love me, don't ask
Me to suffer by myself. If I'm honest, bereave me. Yet don't leave me
All together; remind me of my mother. On one hand, I re-remember
That brief touch. And one hand's enough. Desire revives in a second,
Like dry milk. Just stir it up. That's not funny
For you but for me, I like mammaries. I'm oedimal, you can just tell
What it is you have to. But me, I need to cross myself
In that tiny vestibule; two fingers move just so
I'm absolved in a bliss annulling all that comes before it. This time
That includes the chair, in which I am upright — in that I am upright.
I *am*. And humble too, as pie. Even now, I shrink myself as that woman
Opens wide, and fingers-first pulls me from the chair, across the table
    top, oh-oh—
Oh, into her mouth.

hot cross bun

Little Jack Horner's thumb
Leaves the pie for a bun. And Mother Goose says: Wrong.
She's jealous. Jack's satisfied.
So's the bun, it being completely licked
From under his nail. It likes to be nailed,
That martyrish bun, as Jack fits the bun to his palm,
The hole in its head is the hole in his hand,
That martyrish Jack. That fascist Jack, that good boy
Plunging his thumb through the vulnerable bun,
Pretending it's dead.
Once up on him, Mother goosed Jack
With a meat thermom— Oh Jack!
Sat in a corner and sulked.
It was Jack who wanted to die.
But martyrish Mother gave him a snack. She said:
I am this milk and this pie.
Nursing rhymes in double time
For his bird-brained mother,
Jack got up, threw pie in her face;
Now he puts the bun in its place.

color by number

You with the reddening face —
Can you identify this body? Please
Classify your remains.
Are they: X.) a dirty pair
Of dice (that's two times
Die) in Eve's sublime-mating
Game where numbers turn up
Bone, or: Y.) the indefinite term
Of your bleary life,
Undistinguished, paled
By dissolutions (you see her now
You don't) and loss
Of limbi?
                if we don't joke about
The dead. So you lost
A relative. You won a lack. That's more
To reckon with. If the tears add up
To unhealable rifts, slashes
Of your knife in your mother's
Wedding dress, a gift
You hated and wanted —
You won't wear it! You won't cry
Out, without thinking first
She can't hear it. And though you never could
Sing as she sang, we have to try
Putting "this" behind "us" — "thus"
                (All set? And three, and four, and —)
You're a textbook illustration
Of how your anatomy
Maps the transparency
You're up against —

Hey baby, relax. The world turns
On its axial tomography. And every
Celluloid needs an Other. The still-photographed
Dead need you. Think of how
She'd tell you not to mope. (Sure, she would —
She *was* your mother, no?) Afraid of multiple
Choice? Or multiple _____? — the act
Of filling in? If so, exactly how many blanks
Do you draw, do you play
With yourself, in recreation
Of the blue tones she drew
Your hazy January breath
Away with, by saying: *Darling, please*
Square your shoulders, and *Love, do try*
To stay inside the lines.

dorothy confesses, gets off, goes free

Throw The Book at me. Hit me again. I swear to tell the Whole Truth, so help me
Oz. Just a girl, I plead inanity. It's Mother's fault. Don't be entranced
By her sweeping entrance into a case where it was written, "Green,

I want you green," and the words made a difference: The grass *is* greener there
But so's her envy — and she's to blame. It's in The Book. Don't miss quotes.
Look beyond the straw man. And quick. Time is money down the drain-

Hole of Tradition. It's the fall in Wonderland. Random repetition:
See exhibit ABC, Dick and Jane, and the rest. That they don't
Suspect me may be suspect. Alice should be watched. In case of pregnancy,

That Rabbit is dead meat. Me, I'm the kitten; she played with
A harmless bawl of tangled yarns. The Whole Truth: Well — I sang so well —
The twister took the rap. But in fact, I killed the witch. OK, I'll start talking,

Straight or not. The house and I were soaring, I couldn't stop.
Someone had to take the heat. I was hot. I confess
She was my mother. And I'm a very loving daughter. Every night I call

The shots, reverse the charges: Ding dong, Mom is chthonic; I'm on top.
Yes, I would kill again; read The Book: She was a wicked lesbian.
"Get reeling," they directed, and ever since I've been projecting.

I'm just a girl, in The Book. In another neverland, however, I'll endeavor
To be a *poetess*. I'll pull myself up higher, lower, onto the face of the witch.
I'll say yes-yes-yes like Miss Mollified blooming from an authoress's lips.

I'm the witch's girl. I'm obsessed with threes. I'll become the house
Itself — in which I bear the death — that which engendered me. I'll fly
Her back to Life. Syntax. Genealogy. We'll explore the double helix of our D&A

And S&M. The double hex. It's what I am: Innate insanity. Ex-implicit complicity.
Yet also three — "For All Eternity" — Oh, Aunty Em, there's no place like —
Mother Emily. Go on — Toss *that* book at me — Yes Yes Yes.

four roses

At least since Freud, De Saussure and Industrial Revolution,
Our world has been rewritten to reveal its repetition
And discontinuity. A changing game that's always lost, a loss which
We desire to be a—*gain*. A rose wasn't a rose; the one before you wasn't you.

But you remind me of her. So I will win and lose you.
You will play the part well, without knowing its name.
The fragile rose is reveiled in its rosy-looking glass,
Hah (hah). Bite my tongue; we'll fantasize a past—*oral love.*

Our separate memories spread out across our skin,
And ripple ever farther from our points of contact, as when two coins
Dropped in water make spreading circles; they intersect, sketch an
    always-fading rose.
Long before these surface circles stop, the money has been lost. We may
    have met

Where our circumferences crossed. The pretense
Of these roses was a rise in your color when I breathed you in.
Above us, a... *bouquet of stars,* just for you. (Hah.) Down here, their counterparts
Hover on the pond's taut skin, in reflections of after-images.

history lessens

letter of explanation

Dear Current Resident:
Congratulations! You have
Never been a conception
In a pure sense. Nothing
Personal but — Know your birth date? Take it
As a combination
Of digits that unlocks
Nil — your fingers twitching, numbers spinning
Without catching; the galvanized bolt
At the core of your corporeity pivoting
To the left, to the right, without any
Definite result, just its zinc coat
Gleaming, or so we write. That's the idea —
Only — we can't actually see any cylinder
In its socket, nor weigh the light
Pulsing from it to your compulsive
Pupil, black hole taking in the stars'
Propagations, their universal
Junk-annunciations. But we're convinced
Wavelengths from what you thought
Was your first moment — that is, from the end
Of your mother's miraculous tunnel —
Must have snaked in and struck
Your metal. We're sure your existence is not
More corporal than poetic, but rather
Concretely noetic — illuminated
In this anno Domini. And you, now,
Read without knowing if you read
These words or other words,
In other words, gleaming, actually, you can't
See the characters that snaked in and struck
The hour that this or anything began: Dear
Friend, We recommend your prompt submission
To our correspondence club. Please note the expiration
Of even Christ's first breath may be exchanged
For any out-of-the-belly "Aaaaa" — a newborn's
Usurpation of the "a" from apple; for thus it is written
That baby "a" may *be* an apple, whose stem uncoils from its arc
And slips straight into "d" in desperation.

self delphinitions

De fine self de
Very fine self in deed
I like a little story to hold me in
Place is a verb if you think
So, there
Is the place, is the distance in "twitch"
I can't go on without stopping
I can't stop without ongoing
Motion, are you moved?
I like something to keep me
Preoccupied, occupant-posted
Are you proCupid?
I only pause for questions
(no) Line reeks
(no) Fools stop
Undergoing perjury,
I'm going under
Occupation, and you too,
I'm *you* two
Times, do
Change: a moving
Defignition —
Are you moved to?
Try this: Eat Mimi,

I'm a hot piece
Of bread, Jesus,
Much can be said, I wine
For a roll with the punch
Lines, poles, sticks —
You thought I was
Circles, holes, abyss —
A "byss" is a cat
In Arabic, my arched back
A parenthesis (my
Curvature, apparent thesis)(
Slangs open, so
Snap me — sap flows
My pubic hair is Velcro
My public heir is me
Yes, this is me —
Oedible
In verse-ion
Speaking, hello?
Adulterers Anonymous?
Next crime, please
Do her in
Phone sex
Clickety clickety clickety
Spilt

please forward

Mr. President, I'm beginning to wonder about our state
Of mind, and wanted you to know
I was thinking, just *thinking*
We might all die in an hour
Should inspire us in an ever-and-anon
Sense: the thought that we could begin "again"
Or "begin" again. When it's all over "begin,"
"Again," and every other word will be pure
Again. We'll have a brand-new being, a historicity
Out of true nothingness, a sure thing.
It's clear we Americans need
Certain verification. *By God,*
Mr. President, it's us or them
Who will have to die after all
That is, after everything
That is, everything metaphorically
Speaking, plainly has turned out
To be turning into
Something else, up to no good, like a wick'd
Candle simply disappearing, burning itself up— rising
Into smoke. That's it, burning
Like the radicals burning flags, burning
To turn the cloth black. Oh, and I do mean
Black, Sir, like ashes, Sir, *black*
As old printers dye
Pushed into the graved
Die to be taken in by some
Porous paper. *By God,* Sir, our constitution's
Full of holes — We're all going to die! Even you and I
May not fully realize our lives
Are best when blest by diversity
In deaths too, and death's only
A metaphorical absolution, nothing
More than a metaphor
Within; and without
Its show of variety, its meandering
Lack of global certainty, life's meaningless if you
Please, Mr. President — *Don't*
You think?

prayer

Leibniz believed in harmony and so did Wagner.
So did Nietzsche, until Wagner wrote to Nietzsche's doctor
Linking Nietzsche's headaches to excessive masturbation.
The letter made Nietzsche rage, for which the only cure
Was to masturbate while singing out of tune
An aria from Wagner's *Flying Dutchman.*
And soon, the universe no longer fit together
As Leibniz thought it should, and worse for him,
Voltaire made mincemeat out of *Monadology.*

So now it's said God is dead, and I for one am terrified
He's playing possum. Remember when Nietzsche tip-toed
To the point of Leibniz's pyramid.
Nietzsche stepped onto the highest monad,
And said, *The abyss! It's awesome!*
And the serpents hissed, *Yes, yes,*
We want Fred. Nietzsche gagged, sensed a split in his tongue
And his lower body. Looking back, Nietzsche mooned Wagner.
Nietzsche said, *God is dead.* But Nietzsche felt

God's watching. And he fell. Let us pray
For a space of our own
In which to masturbate, and to hate
And to love without retraction
My clitoris, its little tongue
That learned so young to lie.
God, your honor, I cannot fell a Truth.
You refuse to forsake me
And this had taken me a long time to grasp. But now I know

My nostrils were opened with a fork,
The fanged hunger of the asp lets me breathe.
I deceive the air itself, I take it in.
My God has not forsaken me,
Though I brush him off with my heart-pointed tail.
God is watching with his one glass eye.
God casts his marble, hits the target.
He will not say goodbye, though each night
I plead impotence; I can only couple with the devil.

Dear God, you and Nietzsche are both vampiric angels,
Sated, immortal. Each month you bleed me.
Bleed me, drink from me.
God, I am your vessel. I want us together
To dry up. Let my surface crack with your absence,
My fingers singe into straw. Let me fly without reproach,
Let me have no faith at all. I wouldn't miss you, then.
I would eat my own flesh. I would love me.
I would love me into dust.

good advice

Have a good day.
Take your architectonic certainty with you. Always remember: Never mind.
Have a bad day.
See it through; trace your signature wherever you're supposed to sign.
Have a good day.
Collect dead letters. Sleep on 'em. Unfold nothing you wouldn't do at home.
Have a bad day.
Airy delivery? Don't jump out the platonic plane. Speak in plain, laconic terms.
Have a good day.
Speak on the plane of Lacanic terms. Get a degree of some kind, maybe certainty.
Have a bad day.
Don't tense; be. — It won't be the same kind of verbalese. Be a kind to animals.
Have a good day.
Learn to love your cliché. Space extends no farther than existence can.
Have a bad day.
So then there's nothing further than the universe, to say, it all stops Here.
Have a good day.
Learn to repeat yourself.

authority, don't give me that archaic smile

Zygote's a word that yokes my things to your thought; Zygote's a classic egghead,
  Laid in the mass marriage of all thoughts to your thing — but it was zygote
Who set the gametes trysting in the spaces of the alphabet, between Y and X,
U & I, M 'n' B. Am I to tell you how to be? Then Mister Master, don't start in
The beginning of "History." Don't open with Apologue. Nor go stickily, stoically,
The way of Zeno's pen — spouting the great white wail of the great white male,
    endangered specious arguments.

You should recall women and slaves had no names, before you mourn the loss
  Of Grecian urns and Western sperms. Accept others' sexuality even if they don't
Miss you; don't shrink back instead into the biased cut of the full skirting
Of issues — your zealous nonchalance turning female, famine and my fantasies
Each into just another "F" word. Sure, I'd also like to get away
    with signing my will "George Eliot," or "John Doe," not some illiterate

XX, double-crossing, evil chromossos. Too many of those can turn a male man
  Into postperson, and may delay our deliverance from Pandora's Packaging.
Hey boys! Just between us, what do you get when you send Mom to med school?
A nurse in provocative dress and over-active xyster! Heh. A misplaced housewife
Sure to try to scrape Dad clean of his white meat, turning wishbone halves
Into halve-nots, lining one side up against the other, to see who's longer,
    giving dark drumsticks infamous, unfair odds in the post-Emancipation

Wilderness. Seriously, woman's hystorical hunger always has made men enemies.
  If we exsect sexism from racism, materialism from maternalism, his-
Isms from her schisms, will we engender us genderless as apples and whole
Some, or all itching to rule the new paradigm of paradise — or, will we choose
    to chew the fat fruit of masterbaiting, exploring copious copulas between

Vaseline and vacillating? At the risk of being plain titillating, let's veer
  Now to McDonald's in Moscow: *Russian bread is leaving town, squashing down,*
  Turning brown, Russian bread is losing ground, to-o-o Mac's seed bun.
  If you can't nuke 'em, coin 'em: Dah-Dahism's back, or so we play. A no-fun
    allopathist, I wouldn't feel giddy enough to tell you any of this

Unless turned impudent by improvidence of new love, Skooby-do love, hoppity hope
  Kneading clipped claws into my skin. Yes, I've met someone. I too want to
  Selfishly sin, to thrall for the fall; forget Africa, we're all famished
  For a ravished-virgin video to get us through the leftovers of our Last Supper,
  Something genuine, touching enough to re-sex Satan, giving us back
    the startling effect of

Testicles, tits and golden asses, on this earth, in this multi-
  Demential world where two is the sum of an advertisement, zero mass
  Or communion, the imaginary line between a couple, straightest, most efficient
  Distance, flat reel-to-reel thrust of prime programming, mildly satisfying
    dependable, expendable

Sex. Yep. My future former lover said, "In the U.S. it's like snacking: You want to
  When you shouldn't; it's good now but then you wish you hadn't. You're afraid
  Already it shows. I'm superstitious, can't believe in anything. I invite you to
  Sing, suspend me in disbelief, send me
    into the ozone

Rocking, O God keep me rocking." The innate in-outs of breathing,
  The ups and downs of oxygen, my heart gasping for fresh blood, my heart
  A metaphor for brain, brain a thing of social privilege, and privilege
  The light that gleams through our teeth and skin, each one of us Anglicans
    a kind of Christmas ornament —

Quisling of the pagan images that occupy all religion
  Of the body or the mind. For example, how we do love the quincunxial
  Arrangement of white butter on coarse black bread, or the quaint, quixotic talk
  Of stopping torture everywhere forever. How we hate silence on the other side
  Of the interrogation lamp; why can't we make them give up
      all pretense of (possibility of) replacing us? Won't you

Please absolve me? — I'd rather script than act, keep my risks abstract
  And my self unilaterally mobile. No one truly loves a do-gooder without a Nobel.
  So anyway I turned to my lover and confessed, "Perfection exists only as opposed
  To pleasure and vices, verses. Which reminds me: Do you have a warranty?
  Remote control? Got to protect my ego and immune system." Okay, I'm about done
  And overdone, poet-hypocrite plying you with play currency of rhyme (See:) Below
      though not above wit. So, love it

Or — Ohhh, skip it, since there's

No sense in going on with the way we've tried to save dolphins and Negroids as if
  Equal matters. You suspect the problem's their attitude, and pray they'll rise up
  In gratitude — Flipper and Uncle Tom grinning and dutiful, while we beautiful
  Big white girls undo our zippers just for you, the free-love platitudes
      melting in our mouths, not in your hands.

M&M smacks of my morosity, and too, man's sweet reluctance to meet the mean
  Truth that beginnings and endings wrinkle in middle age. We should pry
  Open letters, ends and 'ands. If we can move, it's elliptically: Curves may turn up
  Down, back, straight, black, white. But, this is "only" allegory, which means...
  That's another story. You know there always is one, and more than one.
      Mmm.

24

femme follies

"self-help," a two-act play

Ladies and gentlemen, let's interact.
Do you suffer from ennui, malaise, and other bouts
Of French? At least in theory? Please allow me
To tell you a little bit about myself: I repeat.
And that's enough. Now, can I have a volunteer
To hold a candle to my pubic hairs —
Stand back!
And now — they cleave to the spaces between my legs!
And now — they cleave the spaces between my legs!
If you can, bare with me. And now —
Watch this: Stick thimbles on my nipples,
A fresh daisy behind;
And you may snap my picture
From any vantage,
You can take it anytime, anywhere
But with you. Cheers! Chers
Mesdames et messieurs —
Help yourselves, to my advantage.
And now, let's tip the big glass,
And toast my slanted image.
Roast any part of me
In the glaze of that gaze —
I remain intact
Yet out of tact, defect
From my reflection. Though on reflection,
I love to effigy. I love to burn
In terror of the mere "or"
Of grammar. Ta daa! —
    I'm not making any sense.
    I'm not making any, since
    I'm making you incensed
In order to force you to re-order
Me, warmed over semantically. And how —
And now — Just be. *Like* me. All together now.
Turn around and around, and everybody chant:
Thou shalt, though shan't —

Until right before your eyes, I can't
Recant blood — letting pleasure
Seep into my pants. I'm a beast.
I pant: Dear boys and gargoyles,
Do you suffer periodical envy? Well, I'll be —
An hibitionist. Is there anything we've missed?
Cut.
Oh, Miss Caste?
May we have a ten-minute inner mission, please?
And now, while we do, won't some of you
Disjoin me for a quick nip at the bar
Or the jugular? My, I like that,
Blood everywhere. I must ask you to have some disrespect.
Be quite a please, and pay a tension
Anything it asks, to come unstrung. We simply have. Act, too.

corner performance, the movie

I want to be alone — Impossible
Outside space/time, I'm poss-
ible, Able, don't quibble
Over lines. I refuse to
Ravel *or* unravel. (What's
Indifference?) I bet heads. I didn't choose to

Grovel face-down like a Penny
With tail upturned. I didn't ask to *be*
Pricked by a diaper's safety pin.
Hey mOm, your hole's in the middle. That's the Law
Of the Excluded Middle. Well,
Press my extra-belly button, then —

B-b-b-b-y the way, folks,
I am NOT a child. Yup, bet I'm better
Off than you, and almost everyone who's ever lived

Since almost all of them are dead,
Since then. My inheritance: this bubbly soap box
And a cup of decoy tin
Dimes — for Kotex, as it turned out: Adolescence,
RETURN OF THE SAFETY PIN.
Inheritance: a stumbling block,
Though I'm sure I'll cotton to it
If I can. Dear audience,
I'd like to ask...
You, you, you, *why* you —

Why *you? I* wouldn't have been
Here ("She's right *there.*")
Without you. Anyway, without a doubt (music starts in)
I'll weather you, whether you
— don't or do —
Doubt I love you. Stained or shrined: Doubt, I love you.

In the flicks, she raises one eyebrow and says, "I *vant* to be alone."
Then again, she says, "Come up and *see* me sometime."

yowling for blood

He said I left blood on his bedspread. He said *stain,* to me
It rhymed with rain. He said "Mother" made the quilt.
Blood veined the seams pulling together
Patches of matter. From this I gathered
She and I will never be the same
As he was once: undivided

Upon a time, man was Man,
In essence purity and light
Bulbs are cracking open — Spring! Spring! —
(Follow those bouncing balls, grammarians.)
Enlightenment: In a sense light
And purity of thought — but individual divides in dual
Parts; it hurts. What's the matter, Patches? I may lick his hand today but then
I've always loved Virginia. Even though she never did like sex,
I learned from her, from her I

        removed two ice;
I drank her blood hot. Without those eyes I saw almost
She re-assembled a warm, welcome Vagina, but not quite: Vrgina.
And then I took the "r" away, even though it's present
Tense! — and the hole where "a" should have been becomes *very* becoming.
"Room of One's Own" — Give me a break. Wash out her mouth,

Efface her face, expose her artifice, orifice, whorlish
Metonymy. Pushing deepest into the latest cliché, I find the reader
So a-textual. So so-so. "You" know "you"
Really will have to lick my best envelopes to find me out
Of town. Control. Or luck. Lick. Letters split like that — Like it. Take it
Back   your tongue   mine will fit
I love you and— We interrupt this—
Announcement: These fragments

Are rags, meant to cover any snatch
Of lost conversation
Or bleeding flesh. I suffer
The lust to be quilled
Into the formal garments
Of moral arguments. Oh the holes in my nylon
Anagrams, my literary wet dreams. Take it, take
My shredded evidence, the taped erasure of my most mo-
lst gap; note that centrally important "I", the hyphenated hy-

Men and women
Long to be re-sown
Together in the blood
Of a child's round emerging head, but instead
We go merrily around a round
Period... wet globe dropping over and over
The edge... repeatedly sinking in
The slinking tails of sentences, just as once a month
I make myself known
By dispelling myself. Stain, rain, stain, rain. It's like changing
A sweaty, stinking para-
Dox.

I love and loathe you. He said. From my very own mouth
This hymeneal hymn, this inside-out ear-
Reverent honeyed mooning
Of the Woolfs, their O so duplicitous,
Lost in a sense, but not so in another
That you'd forget yourself, dear reader, dear
Dear reader. Say *Leonard*. Say *Virginia*. Say *Leonard*. Say *Virgin*—
Bleed, unleash yourself.

now, now, he said, but medea replied:

I want to undo this peace that reigns
In our house, that reins in
My desire for violence, my wish
Like an object in space, colorless as Venus's
Absent arms; meteorite and marbled muscles striking
Sparks, the idea helluva lot brighter
Than real material. Even at sunrise, my sky opening

Into a last night; I hallucinate the stars, what's really there
Matters nothing, until light-years from now
I'll guess who we are Now,
Now, you say, but my right
Eye shuts till the future,
My left ear tunes to the past. (Nonsense to you? I'm doing
The female feint, the off-center cross-stitch;
Look out for your crotch-stick.)
Look in my mouth for the mmmm
Of the immanent present, but if you look now

You won't hear it: Darlin',
Time don't stop to talk.
(Chorus: Nothing matters.) Time takes all
As having been imminent. Yet, time *does* take the cake-
Walk back. I transgress
This time, a prophetess; the whole omen
Like the hole in women: Truth is death. Without no eminent

Phallic yardstick, I measure it
In terms that'll come to pass. I cast
Venus's arm out of Alice's
Glass, to do the task. But you win again.
You, too, wanted to outlive the children.

domestic bliss

> He stuck in his thumb, pulled out a plum
> And said, "What a good boy am I!"

Phhh. Testing,
Testing. Speaking, leaking
Rhythmic Inc.
Corporated, R-rated
Corpses.... Who? Sez who? Analysis, paralysis,
Phthisis of my finger, and the thumb
I used to write with
Aplomb, in good taste — a plum
Pit stuck now between my teeth.
An old nursery rhymed.
But that feast is over, and the seed
Forces me to lisp — plump pith
Dissolved into a memory, sucked-up
Satisfaction I imagine
With the plumber.... Well, I *never*
Did *that* with the plumber. So
Tell them all it's time:
The milkman, repairman, mailman, painter.
I want them *now,* in my entryway.
I guess you all wonder
Why I've asked you here tonight.
You, the very mailman, please stamp
My forehead with a letter.
You, the repairman, please fix me
Up with the milkman. I'm thirsty
For my mama's breast, and it's the next best thing
To get it from the painter,
Who's doing the interior,
Since the neighbors might look in. So lock us in,
Bible salesman, in your hard brief case
History of this lady of the house.

Does it state what state she's in, her crazy, anal
-ytic sense of humor? Mind your p's and q's
In "**p**lumber" and "**p**ainter"; their gallant dual
Absence of the p's mirror image
Is a double negative. That's a positive, a good
Cue; don't miss your opening
To question any noun's gender. Plumber, painter —
What's in a name? Take the missus;
Paint her, plumb her, ain't she still the same? Are you a plumb
Confused kinda reader? Ever read her
Red hair as something other than a hot sort of color? Ever
Ask who you are, and why, who'm I, and why
I rudely intimate her wet, crudely intimate pleasures
Will get executed plum by plum with the microphone on
The floor of your foyer.... Phhhhhhh.

which is right?

Each writer knows she is born of another like herself. Daughter, mother. Yet who is the third party? Professor Amoritis suggests: Is it not some great man of Romantic sensibility? And responds with a certain "yes." But in questioning herself, the authoress puts her finger on the problem — and her finger disappears; her triangular "3" has once again opened its misshapen box, riting, riting, riting

A Brew **"Re•ci•pe**

[imperative of *recipere* to take] anything proposed as
a remedy, for doing something, or for producing a desired result."

Use fresh or thawed
Fowl. It will smell
Sharp and feel almost
Like a baby, her skin
Tough — or, if that doesn't suit you,
A man, his skin
Prickled, hot under your hot
Water. Blot
Beneath the arms
And severed neck. Salt,
Allow absorption, and resalt;
Now imagine: If you choose
To stew a whole body,
Called a genre, [*genus*], gender
Of the source indicates a pinch
More for those old birds
You must pluck stubbornest
Quills from. Cook. When the flesh
Crackles, recall every life
Means another death. Place a wizened apple
In the space where once
Was a mouth. To make it speak, add new tongue
Of calf. Fold in just enough
Coherence to put the old rose-colored

Flaps in back of you: They bore you
Upward. By rote
They went: you go
Off disparately —

Cock a doodle, do.
Rock and diddle, too.
Flap, flap, flap.

this is just a fairy tale

And it's for the ladies:
Beside Moses, a basket-case, Miriam
Waits. In the bull rushes.
Off with her outfit, and she's Europa
Getting it backwards
From Zeus. — Moses or Minos, Mary or Pasiphae,
It's the same rose-cheeked girl, same snow-white bull
Reforming, never reformed, remanifested
In each manifesto. Some guy always takes her.
Jesus or Jung or Mao Tse Tung. Let's memorize
Mesmerization, study the angles as well as angels;
Let's fall apart and together like Tinkerbell Toys —
Come on, girls! Let's abandon the boys.

citizen jane

I'm feeling Hitlerish, mixed up
With a country;
My vagina's Germany.
Naw, I'm faking being
Frau Fraud, Faux Freud.
Too many "F"-ing capitals
Make me lose control.
Urination? I like it.
But we're a nation too,
So as for me and mind
You, patriotism's our common
Dildon't, while personal perversion's
A redundancy. My hip's "in"
An orgy of mass hysteria.
And private privates is
An oxymoron or on
The other foot, it's not
Something one can truly rule.
We're all in continents.
There's no more unexplored dry land
To stamp down on. You can kick around
A snooty fetish like a foot ball.
It becomes a smutty, garish
Habit of the masses,
The way the sixties passes
For the end of uh linear narrative.
And lasses in sun dresses
Become bitches in heat
Without relief, without background
To project themselves from,
And so, just like that, fall in
To dangling modifiers of
The same old sexuality. Lines never really break
Down. Do they? Please
Pee on me.

mr. america visits sex—surrogate miss history; she says:

Try to relax. It's natural to fantasize about doing it
To the dead. Screw taboo.
Join me? One pain-killer aphrodisiac
Or two? Slide back the cover
Of my wooden box:
Powdered instant innocence. Go ahead,
Sniff. The centuries didn't exist — no
Indians, Coloreds, Jews,
Japanese — except to give you
                FREEDOM TO CHOOSE
These: Take a few
Inhalations of the enclosed snuffs, and it'll seem as if
It's all over it's all over it's all over
Some steeply sloping interstate, we're swerving fast enough
Over bumps so that our giddy guts lighten
Up, and up, until they're overhead, comic
Caption balloons, white vacancies, letting us
Down (good for you now?) by the tips
Of our tongues. Falling flat, across paper
As we fall too, those dumb little
Stick words yell POW! CRACK! AIEE! I think it'll
Be some time before you wake from this — it'll be just
The two of us, lying apart
Of it all, you know, or from it all, like, whatever
Heirs you lost stuck forever in my wall-to-wall.
Sure, progress is over. Oh, bugger the young.
It's late. No, it's early, whoops, I neglected your breakfast
And your fingerprints — Press here, dear. Sure, we're almost done, and if
   you should feel
A thing, just rewind to where I remind you: *Time for our medicine.*

rhymal stream

Roll in the clover over a lover that's me
Playing. Come say with my words.
Get juicy with me.
I'm a textual lymphomaniac.
I love your fluidity.
Get that spring back in your body.
Suck a thumb and wet the page thumbing
Your run-on nose.
Piss with your diction. Pissing's
Alchemy, and anyway,
Someone'll change your dirty hyper-
Ventilated aspirations. Take me
For a ride before someone else
Kicks your gall between the dregs
Of a last drought. Don't leave the well
Enough alone, especially if the tone
Is dry.

pussycat

Purring to a dialectic, pleasure's a pain
In the ass. The sheet on my bed
Folds in half; there's two sides to everything.
I can't decide... if you know what I mean.
I've simply only just — Deary me! —
Parried a dichotomous thrust. I use the doggy's
Double edge to pare myself down
And flirty. Dreary me, all alone,
I've paired "my" to "self"; my self's possessed —
The devil sleeps in my anus.
When he snores, I fart. The devil gives me a bad sense,
Humors and smell. I'm acting up
To anyone's standards. I act down too.
My feline's feral. Meow. Hiss. Me: *ow*. (His *S*.)
I like to catch snakes. It's natural.
I like to invite Freudian readings,
Then neglect to make din-din
Or stay home. But if I did greet them,
I'd show them my anus. That's a friendly thing
For cats; that's empirical fact.
My breasts are imperial fat, my nipples tiaras.
I'm a queen wasp; that's sociological truth.
That's a logical spoof on a racy image.
I try to make the top dogs pay for it.
I prostitute so as not to bore you
How they bore me, through. And through. Oooh. It's either or
Or and. Prostate slash prostrate. Slash slash slash.
I'm male and female.
My balls are detachable. Two of my teats are tickled pink.
Cats have six. Cats have sex, but the females don't like it.
That's what the experts think. I know better, though.
I've always known better, and it's never stopped me.

shift: a woman's chemise or a dress

On the bathroom wall: Hey
Men! Look up Zeugma* and me —
We'll make it worth your while.
To pass the hours and yours,
I've changed my style
To shifty eyes and lip.
Well, it's about time
And space. No, it's only about
Midnight, in my princess-met-a-text,
The moment I take off
My dress to give you the slip,
And the femme shimmies up,
Making you a milk toast.
This could happen any split
Second, at any given take
On sex; every verb for it's
Zeugmatic,
Making three points:
3.) me, desiring,
2.) an ever-reseeding addictive ideal
And I.) a substitute that dissatisfies the real — "I"
Want to possess "you" and inappropriately, "you."
Once upon a crime
(I'm not mouthing mere formula)
Isis slipped myth-to-math into isosceles;
I + You = One, Two,
Many breasts.
A breast must have been my first love,
But even it already had a double,
And between them a gap/gaff\laugh, go
Ahead. Freud waxed his mustache
But not enough on his lack
Of mammaries and that lactation complex.
My mother was convex — and yet a fetish?
A mirror-glass slipper? Hmmmph.
Daddy concaved into depravity
Though the bottle didn't become him.
(But enough so that I wanted it.)
The confusion's so slippery,
I compulsively bend at the waste.
(I almost drown, reaching down

In the Freudian, see?)
I become an odd bottle shape,
Another fetish: Ho, I'm a scream,
Scrawl, scroll stuffed in the throat
Of a self afloat. That's why you find me here and now
So insatiable.
(_____ me. Let me _____ you.)   you   you   you   you
          milk
I want to stop.
I want to unstop.
I'm a bottleneck of Grimm tales.
Lost Little Red Childhood,
An early period. My parents' pumpkin
Holds a candle for them both.
OK, I'm duplicitous and hollow
To internalize Cinderella. Why not let it slide.
Digestion's a forked (tongue-
Twisting) gestation, and
It's always midnight somewhere
As long as somewhere shifts.
I can always switch a definition for a change,
A princess for a drag queen, perhaps
A shift of clothes, no less —
But more, it's about redressing.
It's about French fashions,
Making the last, "a-hem," line last
Beyond Lacan, doubling
Up with laughter, cough-cough, lovers —
Zeugmas, "typical" "triple plays"
In male terms though it puts them out. I always come
About through improper attachments.
It's about a bout of shrifting: Oh fathers, do forgive us
Our weaknesses and strengths,
And for sometimes being straight with you.
Ahem, pardonnez-moi. You're in the Ladies Room.

*zeug•ma (zōōg'mə), n. Gram., Rhet. the use of a verb with two subjects or objects
(or of an adjective with two nouns) although appropriate to only one of the two, as
in to wage war and peace.

43

four sextettes

the impasse rides again

At the impasse, fellas, this posable ladder unfolds from out of my pocket
Dictionary, and snaps into space. If you cross words under it, it's bad luck,
Which is better than none. The ladder links shake with weight, tenuous as lips
Saying "sensuous." Link shake with weight — and see, the old links break.
So many ways to read my links, take my lips, speak without being broken to
Fragments. I break just like a little buoy. The hot air pops open
And I sink like a fallen woman. Do you remember the Muzak I do? I was borne
On the year '58 all the way to '59, and then I got out and hailed another.
Could be when you think of ladder, you think of fire; fire reminds me of water,
How it flickers between my legs when I masturbate in the bath. Free association
Has its price. So I may sell you a piece of a bridge or a ladder. Heidegger
Didn't know the West is an ongoing adventure. This bridge is posed over a dearth
Of knowable earth. The ladder is poised to fall when the "I" falls.
Fellas, what are we getting into? What are we getting out of
This pursuit of fleeting fleeing, a new meaning? If I'm out front, riding
You and you're reading me fast, you won't be embarrassed to be bare-assed.
Together like this we're effable, pardner. You could say that,
And it means a lot, and that's all. Bridge my ladder and the latter pullulates
Improperly from a (apogamy) almost to the end of the alphabet. Y? I don't know
Any other language well enough to do this with; even fellatio's not an issue
Of shyness but of embracing enough to let go, spreading asexually or
   chaotically translated
Disease with disease. Let fugitives go. How we kiss then issue words
Suggests jests are in order. And order's hard to get out of; you have to throw
Out the reposed ladder then go after it, make it disposable at the last second
Chance.

my idle idyll essence

Beep beeep. Move over Dr. Seuss, Derrida and other pipsqueaks. *Beep beeeep.*
This is not a car horn. This is not representational. This is not a test.
At the tone, please drop all your defenses. Ladies, that includes your menses;
Gentlemen, your pants. Children must be accompanied by an adulterer or other old
Joke. My rate's cheap, more minute by the minute. I charge for every second
Coming, I'm un-subtling. Did you know that Jesus is the Son of Santa;
It's in a hidden clause of his conception. God couldn't bear children
Or not to have them. Hey, whatsa matter, had her at tea? Too sophisticated for a
Fist o' katydids? Rip the legs off adolescence. Keep the incidence of crime down
And dirty. Spelling bee: insect or incest? The law protects only families'
Fantasies. Fuck Foucault; you know you want to. He's even better dead —
Isn't that what he said? A self-respecting poet writes herself out of business,
Like any conscientious whore. That's why we can't. There's always more
Where that blame's from. I don't believe in menopause 'cause I never had it.
I bleed like a stuck prig. I sniff at dirt. Hey FBI: I rut for bugs
Because I'm into wired sects. Hey FYI: I'd like to bite you
Where it spurts. I'd like to lap-lap in your lap. Make yourself uncomfortable.
I'll tell you fast: I grew up white and middle-class in a house in rural Indiana.
Nevertheless, puberty was like living in a condom. My left nipple has a hard-on
Just thinking what the right one would have liked in 7th grade. But I never met
The right one. Violence ingratiates itself, like an easy pun I don't trust
But invite back. Why deny it? Well, for one there's always entertainment,
For another, always pain. To "disparage" means to marry down.
If I were a couple, I'd divorce myself to look for someone better
Bred and trained. One hand beats the other as if it were a horse
Too dead to run. Still, I'll gambol on it till I'm broke, since it's a strong-legged
Split in myself I've put my finger on.

crap-trap

Every poetic act is a crap-shooting arc into the dark, if the dark's what you
Happen into. Me, I don't believe in the ark, though thank God it saved the aardvark
From becoming alphabet soup, or we wouldn't have a pig to rhyme with.
Everyone loves a consensus, the natural convergence of disparate lines, like a
Religion, or wrinkly anus. Ever wonder what's the right perspective, right angle
Or 180 degrees? Now you're getting warm. Warmer, warmer, only trouble is
I forgot to hide a thing. Why not just get warm for its own pleasure?
I announce before all, life is not a game. Though after all, it is. It's?
Frank, my dear, I've already lost questions in the interest
Of everyone. Let's drop them, shall we? The balls? No, yes, let it go. I'll find my own
Asshole. Alternate consensi, sense I: Left, right, like a little march
Or big April rain. I'm getting wet. What if there *is* satisfaction
But we want to be dissatisfied? Our essence is not the Lacanian lack
Of any essence, but the famous Ode b'Anal. Excuse my stench.
I know what's what and what's snot. Nose or anus. I think of mine
As getting wet, warm. Are you hiding something? Just who are you *for*
Getting? Getty? Or Pope Jean Paul? Either way, give me all the money.
Please approach the altar native to the present Logos. Please kneel down
By degrees. Let's have a look-see, shall we? Goody, I'll play Doctor God.

criminal confession

I'm going to deposition myself for you, John Q. See, this is how it works:
A pettifogger flogged her with a petty metaphor; so she had to rhyme or season
Lines with sillicisms. Yeah, I claim poetic lices just to bug you, make you itch
To hatch (a hole in a submarine). Take my vice. To be borne again to your
    fondest mammaries,
Dismember everything others have remembered, until there's almost no
    body left,
No limbs to walk out on. We all need something to abandon, so this strategy
Doesn't work, throw it out the door. See, it flies awhile then plays drowned.
The trick is in the seedy shape of it, the hull a fluid metaphor. Vessel, Jet,
Womb, Supertheory. The flying sauce of mass banality goes with everything
Eventually. So if it's all the same, we'll begin again. Put your eye to the
    hatch, your ear
To my ear, and hear the ocean whore. Corn 'n' porn are the products of
    mid-Westerns,
Not my personality. I don't own one anyway. So take my life. I sub and cob
With a paddle on the surface. "I'm sorry." Down deep, I'm just a
    reincarcerated incarnation,
Locked in by a sentence with no key paragraph. Self-indention's passé. So
    we're stuck, maybe.
Okay, I'm a lifer, and in the pen, every poem is a bio, hee hee, degradable.
    Put me down, pal,
Or enter the confessional. My predilection is to start over. It all comes out
    in the wash, so to speak
Is harmless. Those are the facts then, to the best of my collection.

bio for jane ransom

Jane Ransom's first book of poetry, *Without Asking* (Story Line Press, 1989) won the Nicholas Roerich prize. Her first novel, *Bye-Bye* (New York University Press, 1997) won the New York University Press Prize for Fiction. She has also been awarded residencies at Yaddo and MacDowell, and poetry fellowships from the New York Foundation for the Arts and the Massachusetts Council of the Arts. She has lived in Madrid, Paris and Puerto Rico, among other places, and now resides in New York.